Easy Air Fryer Cookbook:

69 Delicious Recipes for Fast and

Healthy Meals.

Table of Contents

Introduction

Have you heard of this amazing kitchen appliance that will literally change your life? I am sure you have! It is a guilt-free and healthy way to enjoy all the fried foods you can imagine. An air fryer circulates extremely hot air, consisting of minuscule oil droplets from your food to give you a soft interior and a crisp and crunchy exterior. An air fryer ignites the Maillard effect which, in short, is a reaction between the sugars and amino acids in your food in the presence of hot air, which leads to elevated flavor and color.

In this e-book you will find all of your queries answered regarding air fryers—and in addition, it provides you with 70+ fantastic air fryer recipes ranging from fries, baked goods, roasted items, and desserts!

This e-book is designed to help busy cooks who spend a majority of their time working or studying. You can be a full-time mom and still struggle to manage the house, kids, and cook healthy food... luckily, your air fryer comes to rescue with its super quick cooking system, and also a healthier way of cooking.

So, let's get started!

Air Fried vs Deep Fried

To air fry your food, all you need is about a teaspoon to a tablespoon of oil compared to deep frying, which mostly requires food to be totally submerged in oil, leading to a higher fat content in food. With an air fryer, you are able to reduce the fat content of a similar deep fried food by up to 75 percent.

Air fry for weight loss

Deep fried foods are well known for their high caloric levels, which make them the number one cause of obesity. One of the reasons why weight loss is a huge challenge is because people get into it for all the right reasons but go about it the wrong way.

Did you know that you can fry potatoes with a tablespoon of olive oil and achieve really tasty French fries?

The point is, with an air fryer, you can include healthy versions of fried foods into your diet plan and still see weight loss results; and because you won't feel deprived, you'll be able to turn your new diet into a really enjoyable lifestyle!

Air Fryer Function

Healthy and user-friendly

An air fryer's cooking chamber emanates heat from a warming component near the food, cooking it all the more proficiently and appropriately. The exhaust fan situated over the cooking chamber provides the required wind current (or airflow) from the underside. This permits the warmed air to continually go through the food. Subsequently, all parts of the food receive a similar warming temperature. Utilizing just a grill and a fan assists the air fryer with blasting warm air at a rapid pace, creating great quality that you will without a doubt discover when eating air fried food.

It is a simple yet creative technique and invention for cooking. Like a rice cooker, an air fryer has a large plate that is removable. It serves you a romantic, tasty, and hot fresh dinner within 15 minutes.

Exhaust system of the air fryer

The exhaust system in an air fryer controls the temperature that is expanded by inner pressure, and discharges additional air as expected to cook the food. The additional air is altogether filtered before being discharged, thus being ideal to nature. Air fryers are both user- and environmentally-safe and odorless.

Benefits of Air Fryer

Healthy food: Air Frying allows you to prepare food using minimum oil, thereby making the food items healthy and low fat. With this method, you will use about 80% less oil than the conventional deep frying method. Not only does it use less oil, but it also enriches the taste of food by making the fried food crispier. Air frying will free you from oil-soaked, gooey fried food.

Multi cuisine: By using the air frying method you can not only fry chips and French Fries, but also fry chicken, vegetables, pakodas, and other fried delicacies.

Uniform cooking: In air frying, food is cooked by circulating a hot stream of air. The hot air circulation helps to cook the food evenly from all sides.

Instant cooking: With air frying, food is fried must faster than it would by using the traditional deep frying method. Food can be fried within a few minutes. You do not have to hover over the fryer, as required in conventional deep frying.

Ease of use and maintenance: Air frying is easier to use and less messy, as the appliance is easy to clean and easy to operate. All you have to do is place the food inside the fryer, switch it on, and relax. The fryer will automatically switch off when it has finished with the frying process. You can leave the food inside the fryer even after it has been switched off without the risk of burning the food. Air fryers also prevent you from inhaling the oil fumes and exhaust gases you would get from traditional fryers.

Cost benefit: Since, the amount of oil, used in air frying is much less, the operating cost automatically decreases when compared to the deep frying method, which needs large amounts of oil for cooking.

Disposing old, leftover oil: In air frying, you do not have the problem of disposing of old oil or storing leftover oil.

Low-fat food: When air frying using the Low-Fat Air Fryer Cooker, frozen food items that need to be baked can be directly taken from the freezer and put right into the air fryer. You only need to adjust the timer and temperature, and the food will be perfectly baked. No need to add any oil. Raw meat also can be cooked using the air frying method without the addition of oil. The hot air circulation makes the meat crispy on the outside and soft and juicy on the inside.

Hands-free cooking: The stirring paddle in an air fryer stirs the food items regularly when air frying. This frees you up for doing other chores while frying is taken care of.

Delicious Recipes

Eggplant Fries

Serves: 6

Cook Time: 10 minutes

Ingredients

- 2 large eggs
- ½ cup grated Parmesan cheese
- ½ cup toasted wheat germ
- 1 tsp Italian seasoning
- ¾ tsp garlic salt
- 1 medium eggplant (about 1-1/4 lbs)

- Cooking spray
- 1 cup meatless pasta sauce, warmed

Directions

1. Preheat air fryer to 400°. In a shallow bowl, whisk eggs. In another shallow bowl, mix cheese, wheat germ, and seasonings.
2. Trim ends of eggplant; cut eggplant lengthwise into ½- inch-thick slices. Cut slices lengthwise into ½-inch strips. Dip eggplant in eggs, then coat with cheese mixture.
3. Spritz eggplant and air fryer basket with cooking spray. Working in batches if needed, place eggplant in a single layer in air fryer basket and cook until golden brown, 5-7 minutes. Turn eggplant; spritz with additional cooking spray. Continue cooking until golden brown, 4-5 minutes. Serve immediately with pasta dipping sauce.

Nutritional Facts:

- Calories: 135
- Fat: 5 g
- Carbohydrates: 15 g
- Protein: 9 g

Raspberry Balsamic Smoked Pork Chops

Serves: 4

Cook Time: 15 minutes

Ingredients

- 2 large eggs
- ¼ cup 2% milk
- 1 cup panko (Japanese) bread crumbs
- 1 cup finely-chopped pecans
- 4 smoked bone-in pork chops (7-1/2 oz each)
- ¼ cup all-purpose flour
- 1/3 cup balsamic vinegar
- 2 TBSP brown sugar

- 2 TBSP seedless raspberry jam
- 1 TBSP thawed frozen orange juice concentrate

Directions

1. Preheat air fryer to 400°. Spritz air fryer basket with cooking spray. In a shallow bowl, whisk together eggs, and milk. In another shallow bowl, toss bread crumbs with pecans.

2. Coat pork chops with flour; shake off excess. Dip in egg mixture, then in crumb mixture, patting to help adhere. Working in batches as needed, place chops in single layer in air fryer basket; spritz with cooking spray.

3. Cook until golden brown, 12-15 minutes, turning halfway through cooking and spritzing with additional cooking spray. Remove and keep warm. Repeat with remaining chops. Meanwhile, place remaining ingredients in a small saucepan; bring to a boil. Cook and stir until slightly thickened, 6-8 minutes. Serve with chops.

Nutritional Facts:

- Calories: 582
- Fat: 36 g
- Carbohydrates: 36 g
- Protein: 32 g

Southern-Style Chicken

Serves: 6

Cook Time: 20 minutes

Ingredients

- 2 cups crushed Ritz crackers (about 50)
- 1 TBSP minced fresh parsley
- 1 tsp garlic salt
- 1 tsp paprika
- ½ tsp pepper
- ¼ tsp ground cumin
- ¼ tsp rubbed sage
- 1 large egg, beaten
- 1 broiler/fryer chicken (3 to 4 lbs), cut up

Directions

1. Preheat air fryer to 375°. Spritz the air fryer basket with cooking spray.

2. In a shallow bowl, mix the first seven ingredients. Place egg in a separate shallow bowl. Dip chicken in egg, then in cracker mixture, patting to help coating adhere. Place a few pieces of chicken in a single layer in the prepared basket, spritz with cooking spray.

3. Cook 10 minutes. Turn chicken and spritz with additional cooking spray; cook until chicken is golden brown and juices run clear, 10-20 minutes longer. Repeat with remaining chicken.

Nutritional Facts:

- Calories: 410
- Fat: 23 g
- Carbohydrates: 13 g
- Protein: 36 g

Fish and Fries

Serves: 4

Cook Time: 25 minutes

Ingredients

- 1 lb potatoes (about 2 medium)
- 2 TBSP olive oil
- ¼ tsp pepper
- ¼ tsp salt

FISH

- 1/3 cup all-purpose flour
- ¼ tsp pepper

- 1 large egg
- 2 TBSP water
- 2/3 cup crushed cornflakes
- 1 TBSP grated Parmesan cheese
- 1/8 tsp cayenne pepper
- ¼ tsp salt
- 1 lb haddock or cod fillets
- Tartar sauce (optional)

Directions

1. Preheat air fryer to 400°. Peel and cut potatoes lengthwise into ½-inch-thick slices; cut slices into ½-inch-thick sticks.

2. In a large bowl, toss potatoes with oil, pepper, and salt. Working in batches as needed, place potatoes in a single layer in air fryer basket; cook until just tender, 5-10 minutes. Toss potatoes in basket to redistribute; continue to cook until lightly browned and crisp, 5-10 minutes longer.

3. Meanwhile, in a shallow bowl, mix flour, and pepper. In another shallow bowl, whisk egg with water. In a third bowl, toss cornflakes with cheese and cayenne. Sprinkle fish with salt; dip into flour mixture to coat both sides; shake off excess. Dip in egg mixture, then in cornflake mixture, pat to help coating adhere.

17

4. Remove fries from the basket; keep warm. Place fish in a single layer in air fryer basket. Cook until fish is lightly browned and just beginning to flake easily with a fork, turning halfway through cooking, 8-10 minutes. Do not overcook. Return fries to the basket to heat through. Serve immediately. If desired, serve with tartar sauce.

Nutritional Facts:
- Calories: 312
- Fat: 9 g
- Carbohydrates: 35 g
- Protein: 23 g

Air Fryer Pickles

Serves: 32
Cook Time: 15 minutes

Ingredients

- 32 dill pickle slices
- ½ cup all-purpose flour
- ½ tsp salt
- 3 large eggs, lightly beaten
- 2 TBSP dill pickle juice
- ½ tsp cayenne pepper
- ½ tsp garlic powder
- 2 cups panko (Japanese) bread crumbs
- 2 TBSP snipped fresh dill

- Cooking spray
- Ranch salad dressing (optional)

Directions

1. Preheat air fryer to 425°. Let pickles stand on a paper towel until liquid is almost absorbed, about 15 minutes.
2. Meanwhile, in a shallow bowl, combine flour, and salt. In another shallow bowl, whisk eggs, pickle juice, cayenne, and garlic powder. Combine panko and dill in a third shallow bowl.
3. Dip pickles in flour mixture to coat both sides; shake off excess. Dip in egg mixture, then in crumb mixture, patting to help coating adhere. Spritz pickles and fryer basket with cooking spray. Working in batches if needed, place pickles in a single layer in basket and cook until golden brown and crispy, 7-10 minutes. Turn pickles; spritz with additional cooking spray. Continue cooking until golden brown and crispy, 7-10 minutes. Serve immediately. If desired, serve with ranch dressing.

Nutritional Facts:
- Calories: 26
- Fat: 1 g
- Carbohydrates: 4 g
- Protein: 1 g

Garlic-Rosemary Brussels Sprouts

Serves: 4

Cook Time: 15 minutes

Ingredients

- 3 TBSP olive oil
- 2 garlic cloves, minced
- ½ tsp salt
- ¼ tsp pepper
- 1 lb Brussels sprouts, trimmed and halved
- ½ cup panko (Japanese) bread crumbs
- 1- ½ tsp fresh rosemary, minced

Directions

1. Preheat air fryer to 350°. Place first 4 ingredients in a small microwave-safe bowl; microwave on high 30 seconds.

2. Toss Brussels sprouts with 2 TBSP oil mixture. Place all the Brussels sprouts in fryer basket and cook 4-5 minutes. Stir sprouts. Continue to air fry until sprouts are lightly browned and near desired tenderness, about 8 minutes longer, stirring halfway through cooking time.

3. Toss bread crumbs with rosemary and remaining oil mixture; sprinkle over sprouts. Continue cooking until crumbs are browned, and sprouts are tender, 3-5 minutes. Serve immediately.

Nutritional Facts:

- Calories: 164
- Fat: 11 g
- Carbohydrates: 14 g
- Protein: 5 g

Spicy Air Fryer Chicken Breasts

Serves: 8

Cook Time: 30 minutes

Ingredients

- 2 cups buttermilk
- 2 TBSP Dijon mustard
- 2 tsp salt
- 2 tsp hot pepper sauce
- 1- ½ tsp garlic powder
- 8 bone-in chicken breast halves, skin removed (8 oz each)
- 2 cups soft bread crumbs
- 1 cup cornmeal

- 2 TBSP canola oil
- ½ tsp poultry seasoning
- ½ tsp ground mustard
- ½ tsp paprika
- ½ tsp cayenne pepper
- ¼ tsp dried oregano
- ¼ tsp dried parsley flakes

Directions
1. Preheat air fryer to 375°. In a large bowl, combine the first five ingredients. Add chicken and turn to coat. Refrigerate, covered, 1 hour or overnight.
2. Drain chicken, discarding marinade. Combine remaining ingredients in a shallow dish and stir to combine. Add chicken, one piece at a time, and turn to coat. Place in air fryer basket sprayed with cooking spray in a single layer.
3. Air fry until a thermometer reads 170°, turning halfway, about 20 minutes. Repeat with remaining chicken. When the last batch of chicken is cooked, return all chicken to the basket and air fry 2-3 minutes longer to heat through.

Nutritional Facts:
- Calories: 552
- Fat: 9 g
- Carbohydrates: 23 g
- Protein: 40 g

Coconut Shrimp and Apricot Sauce

Serves: 6

Cook Time: 10 minutes

Ingredients

- 1- ½ lbs uncooked large shrimp
- 1- ½ cups sweetened shredded coconut
- ½ cup panko (Japanese) bread crumbs
- 4 large egg whites
- 3 dashes Louisiana-style hot sauce
- ¼ tsp salt
- ¼ pts pepper
- ½ cup all-purpose flour

SAUCE

- 1 cup apricot preserves
- 1 tsp cider vinegar
- ¼ tsp crushed red pepper flakes

Directions

1. Preheat air fryer to 375°. Peel and devein shrimp, leaving tails on.
2. In a shallow bowl, toss coconut with bread crumbs. In another shallow bowl, whisk egg whites, hot sauce, salt, and pepper. Place flour in a third shallow bowl.
3. Dip shrimp in flour to coat lightly; shake off excess. Dip in egg white mixture, then in coconut mixture, patting to help coating adhere.
4. Spray fryer basket with cooking spray. Working in batches as needed, place shrimp in a single layer in basket. Cook 4 minutes; turn shrimp and continue cooking until coconut is lightly browned and shrimp turn pink, another 4 minutes.
5. Meanwhile, combine sauce ingredients in a small saucepan; cook and stir over medium-low heat until preserves are melted. Serve shrimp immediately with sauce.

Nutritional Facts:

- Calories: 410
- Fat: 9 g
- Carbohydrates: 60 g
- Protein: 24 g

Bourbon Bacon Cinnamon Rolls

Serves: 8

Cook Time: 10 minutes

Ingredients

- 8 bacon strips
- ¾ cup bourbon
- 1 tube (12.4 oz) refrigerated cinnamon rolls with icing
- ½ cup chopped pecans
- 2 TBSP maple syrup
- 1 tsp fresh gingerroot, minced

Directions

1. Place bacon in a shallow dish; add bourbon. Seal and refrigerate overnight. Remove bacon and pat dry; discard bourbon.

2. In a large skillet, cook bacon in batches over medium heat until nearly crisp but still pliable. Remove to paper towels to drain. Discard all but 1 tsp of drippings.

3. Preheat air fryer to 350°. Separate dough into eight rolls, reserving icing packet. Unroll spiral rolls into long strips; pat dough to form 6 x 1-inch strips. Place one bacon strip on each strip of dough, trimming bacon as needed; reroll, forming a spiral. Pinch ends to seal. Repeat with remaining dough. Transfer four rolls to the air fryer basket; cook 5 minutes. Turn rolls over and cook until golden brown, about 4 minutes.

4. Meanwhile, combine pecans, and maple syrup. In another bowl, stir ginger together with contents of icing packet. In same skillet, heat remaining bacon drippings over medium heat. Add pecan mixture; cook, stirring frequently, until lightly toasted, 2-3 minutes.

5. Drizzle half of icing over warm cinnamon rolls; top with half of pecans. Repeat to make a second batch.

Nutritional Facts:

- Calories: 267
- Fat: 14 g
- Carbohydrates: 28 g
- Protein: 5 g

Chocolate Chip Oatmeal Cookies

Serves: 6

Cook Time: 10 minutes

Ingredients

- 1 cup butter, softened
- ¾ cup sugar
- ¾ cup packed brown sugar
- 2 large eggs
- 1 tsp vanilla extract
- 3 cups quick-cooking oats
- 1- ½ cups all-purpose flour

- 1 package (3.4 oz) instant vanilla pudding mix
- 1 tsp baking soda
- 1 tsp salt
- 2 cups (12 oz) semisweet chocolate chips
- 1 cup chopped nuts

Directions

1. Preheat air fryer to 350°. Line the air fryer basket with foil.
2. In a large bowl, cream butter, and sugars until light and fluffy. Beat in eggs and vanilla. Combine the oats, flour, dry pudding mix, baking soda, and salt; gradually add to creamed mixture and mix well. Stir in chocolate chips and nuts.
3. Form into balls using one TBSP of dough; flatten slightly. Place shaped dough 2 inches apart onto the foil-lined air fryer basket. Air fry for 8-10 minutes or until lightly browned. Remove to wire racks. Repeat with remaining dough.

Nutritional Facts:

- Calories: 102
- Fat: 5 g
- Carbohydrates: 13 g
- Protein: 2 g

Bagel Chicken Strips

Serves: 4

Cook Time: 15 minutes

Ingredients

- 1 day-old everything bagel, torn
- ½ cup panko (Japanese) bread crumbs
- ½ cup grated Parmesan cheese
- ¼ tsp crushed red pepper flakes
- ¼ cup butter, cubed
- 1 lb chicken tenderloins
- ½ tsp salt

Directions

1. Preheat air fryer to 400°. Pulse torn bagel in a food processor until coarse crumbs form. Place ½ cup bagel crumbs in a shallow bowl; toss with panko, cheese, and pepper flakes (discard or save remaining bagel crumbs for another use).

2. In a microwave-safe shallow bowl, microwave butter until melted. Sprinkle chicken with salt. Dip in warm butter, then coat with crumb mixture, patting to help adhere. Spray air fryer basket with cooking spray. Place chicken in a single layer in air fryer basket.

3. Working in batches if needed, cook 7 minutes; turn chicken over. Continue cooking until coating is golden brown and chicken is no longer pink, 7-8 minutes. Serve immediately.

Nutritional Facts:

- Calories: 270
- Fat: 13 g
- Carbohydrates: 8 g
- Protein: 30 g

Green Tomato BLT

Serves: 4

Cook Time: 15 minutes

Ingredients

- 2 medium green tomatoes (about 10 oz)
- ½ tsp salt
- ¼ tsp pepper
- 1 large egg, beaten
- ¼ cup all-purpose flour
- 1 cup panko (Japanese) bread crumbs
- ½ cup reduced-fat mayonnaise

35

- 2 green onions, finely chopped
- 1 tsp snipped fresh dill or ¼ tsp dill weed
- 8 slices whole wheat bread, toasted
- 8 cooked center-cut bacon strips
- 4 Bibb or Boston lettuce leaves

Directions

1. Preheat air fryer to 350°. Spritz basket with cooking spray. Cut tomato into eight slices, about ¼-inch-thick each. Sprinkle tomato slices with salt and pepper. Place egg, flour, and bread crumbs in separate shallow bowls. Dip tomato slices in flour, shaking off excess, then dip into egg, and finally into bread crumb mixture, patting to help adhere.

2. Working in batches as needed, place tomato slices in air fryer basket in a single layer; spritz with cooking spray. Cook until golden brown, 8-12 minutes turning halfway, spritzing with additional cooking spray. Remove and keep warm; repeat with remaining tomato slices.

3. Meanwhile, mix mayonnaise, green onions, and dill. Layer each of four slices of bread with two bacon strips, one lettuce leaf, and two tomato slices. Spread mayonnaise mixture over remaining slices of bread; place over top. Serve immediately.

Nutritional Facts:

- Calories: 390
- Fat: 17 g
- Carbohydrates: 45 g
- Protein: 16 g

Herb and Cheese-Stuffed Burgers

Serves: 4

Cook Time: 15 minutes

Ingredients

- 2 oz cheddar cheese, sliced
- 2 green onions, thinly sliced
- 2 TBSP fresh parsley, minced
- 4 tsp Dijon mustard, divided
- 3 TBSP dry bread crumbs

- 2 TBSP ketchup
- ½ tsp salt
- ½ tsp dried rosemary, crushed
- ¼ tsp dried sage leaves
- 1 lb lean ground beef (90% lean)
- 4 hamburger buns, split

OPTIONAL TOPPINGS

- Lettuce leaves
- Tomato slices

Directions

1. Preheat air fryer to 375°. In a small bowl, mix green onions, parsley, and 2 tsp mustard. In another bowl, mix bread crumbs, ketchup, seasonings, and remaining 2 tsp mustard. Add beef to bread crumb mixture; mix lightly but thoroughly.

2. Shape mixture into eight thin patties. Place sliced cheese in center of four patties; spoon green onion mixture over cheese. Top with remaining patties, pressing edges together firmly, taking care to seal completely.

3. Place burgers in a single layer in air fryer basket. Working in batches as needed, air fry 8 minutes; flip and continue cooking until a thermometer reads 160°, 6-8 minutes longer. Serve burgers on buns, with toppings if desired, add tomato slices, lettuce, and mayonnaise.

Nutritional Facts:

- Calories: 370
- Fat: 14 g
- Carbohydrates: 29 g
- Protein: 29 g

Lemon Slice Sugar Cookies

Serves: 12

Cook Time: 10 minutes

Ingredients

- ½ cup unsalted butter softened
- 1 package (3.4 oz) instant lemon pudding mix
- ½ cup sugar
- 1 large egg
- 2 TBSP 2% milk
- 1- ½ cups all-purpose flour
- 1 tsp baking powder
- ¼ tsp salt

ICING

- 2/3 cup confectioners' sugar
- 2 to 4 tsp lemon juice

Directions

1. In a large bowl, cream butter, pudding mix, and sugar until light and fluffy. Beat in egg and milk. In another bowl, whisk flour, baking powder, and salt; gradually beat into creamed mixture.
2. Divide dough in half. On an lightly-floured surface, shape each into a 6-inch-long roll. Wrap and refrigerate 3 hours or until firm.
3. Preheat air fryer to 325°. Unwrap and cut dough crosswise into ½-inch slices. Place slices in a single layer in foil-lined fryer basket. Cook until edges are light brown, 8-12 minutes. Cool in basket 2 minutes. Remove to wire racks to cool completely. Repeat with remaining dough.
4. In a small bowl, mix confectioners' sugar, and enough lemon juice to reach a drizzling consistency. Drizzle over cookies. Let stand until set.

Nutritional Facts:

- Calories: 110
- Fat: 4 g
- Carbohydrates: 17 g
- Protein: 1 g

Peppermint Lava Cakes

Serves: 4

Cook Time: 15 minutes

Ingredients

- 2/3 cup semisweet chocolate chips
- ½ cup butter, cubed
- 1 cup confectioners' sugar
- 2 large eggs
- 2 large egg yolks
- 1 tsp peppermint extract
- 6 TBSP all-purpose flour
- 2 TBSP finely crushed peppermint candies (optional)

Directions

1. Preheat air fryer to 375°. In a microwave-safe bowl, melt chocolate chips and butter for 30 seconds; stir until smooth. Whisk in confectioners' sugar, eggs, egg yolks, and extract until blended. Fold in flour.

2. Generously grease and flour four 4-oz ramekins; pour batter into ramekins. Do not overfill. Place ramekins in fryer basket; cook until a thermometer reads 160° and edges of cakes are set, 10-12 minutes. Do not overcook.

3. Remove from oven; let stand 5 minutes. Carefully run a knife around sides of ramekins several times to loosen cake; invert onto dessert plates. Sprinkle with crushed candies. Serve immediately.

Nutritional Facts:

- Calories: 563
- Fat: 36 g
- Carbohydrates: 55 g
- Protein: 7 g

Peach Bourbon Wings

Serves: 18
Cook Time: 15 minutes

Ingredients

- ½ cup peach preserves
- 1 TBSP brown sugar
- 1 garlic clove, minced
- ¼ tsp salt
- 2 TBSP white vinegar
- 2 TBSP bourbon
- 1 tsp cornstarch
- 1- ½ tsp water
- 2 lbs chicken wings

Directions

1. Preheat air fryer to 400°. Place preserves, brown sugar, garlic, and salt in a food processor; process until blended. Transfer to a small saucepan. Add vinegar and bourbon; bring to a boil. Reduce heat; simmer, uncovered, until slightly thickened, 4-6 minutes.

2. In a small bowl, mix cornstarch and water until smooth; stir into preserve mixture. Return to a boil, stirring constantly; cook and stir 1-2 minutes or until thickened. Reserve ¼ cup sauce for serving.

3. Using, a sharp knife, cut through the two joints on each chicken wing; discard wing tips. Spray air fryer basket with cooking spray. Working in batches as needed, place wing pieces in a single layer in air fryer basket.

4. Cook 6 minutes; turn and brush with preserve mixture. Return to air fryer, and cook until brown and juices run clear, 6-8 minutes longer. Remove and keep warm. Repeat with remaining wing pieces. Serve wings immediately with reserved sauce.

Nutritional Facts:

- Calories: 79
- Fat: 3 g
- Carbohydrates: 7 g
- Protein: 5 g

Reuben Calzones

Serves: 4

Cook Time: 15 minutes

Ingredients

- 1 tube (13.8 oz) refrigerated pizza crust
- 4 slices Swiss cheese
- 1 cup sauerkraut, rinsed and well-drained
- ½ lb cooked corned beef, sliced
- Salad dressing

Directions

1. Preheat air fryer to 400°. Spritz air fryer basket with cooking spray. On an lightly-floured surface, unroll

pizza crust dough and pat into 12-inch squares. Cut into 4 squares.

2. Layer one slice of the cheese and a fourth of the sauerkraut and corned beef diagonally over half of the each square to within a ½ inch of edges. Fold 1 corner over filling to the opposite corner, forming a triangle; press edges with a fork to seal.

3. Place 2 calzones in a single layer in greased fryer basket.

4. Cook until calzones are golden brown, 8-12 minutes, flipping halfway through cooking. Remove and keep warm; repeat with remaining calzones. Serve with salad dressing.

Nutritional Facts:
- Calories: 430
- Fat: 17 g
- Carbohydrates: 50 g
- Protein: 21 g

Rosemary Sausage Meatballs

Serves: 24

Cook Time: 15 minutes

Ingredients

- 2 TBSP olive oil
- 4 garlic cloves, minced
- 1 tsp curry powder
- 1 large egg, lightly beaten
- 1 jar (4 oz) diced pimientos, drained
- ¼ cup dry bread crumbs
- ¼ cup fresh parsley, minced
- 1 TBSP fresh rosemary, minced

- 2 lbs bulk pork sausage
- Pretzel sticks (optional)

Directions

1. Preheat air fryer to 400°. In a small skillet, heat oil over medium heat; sauté garlic with curry powder until tender, 1-2 minutes. Cool slightly.
2. In a bowl, combine egg, pimientos, bread crumbs, parsley, rosemary, and garlic mixture. Add sausage; mix lightly but thoroughly.
3. Shape into 1- ¼-inch balls. Place in a single layer in fryer basket; cook until lightly browned and cooked through, 7-10 minutes. Remove and keep warm; repeat with remaining meatballs, if needed. If desired, serve with pretzels.

Nutritional Facts:

- Calories: 96
- Fat: 7 g
- Carbohydrates: 2 g
- Protein: 4 g

Wasabi Crab Cakes

Serves: 24

Cook Time: 10 minutes

Ingredients

- 1 medium sweet red pepper, finely chopped
- 1 celery rib, finely chopped
- 3 green onions, finely chopped
- 2 large egg whites
- 3 TBSP reduced-fat mayonnaise
- ¼ tsp prepared wasabi
- ¼ tsp salt

- 1/3 cup, plus ½ cup dry bread crumbs, divided
- 1- ½ cups lump crabmeat, drained
- Cooking spray

SAUCE
- 1 celery rib, chopped
- 1/3 cup reduced-fat mayonnaise
- 1 green onion, chopped
- 1 TBSP sweet pickle relish
- ½ tsp prepared wasabi
- ¼ tsp celery salt

Directions

1. Preheat air fryer to 375°. Spritz fryer basket with cooking spray. Combine first 7 ingredients; add 1/3 cup bread crumbs. Gently fold in crab.

2. Place remaining bread crumbs in a shallow bowl. Drop heaping tablespoonfuls of crab mixture into crumbs. Gently coat and shape into ¾-inch-thick patties. Working in batches as needed, place crab cakes in a single layer in basket. Spritz crab cakes with cooking spray. Cook until golden brown, 8-12 minutes, carefully turning halfway through cooking and

spritzing with additional cooking spray. Remove and keep warm. Repeat with remaining crab cakes.

3. Meanwhile, place sauce ingredients in food processor; pulse 2 or 3 times to blend or until desired consistency is reached. Serve crab cakes immediately with dipping sauce.

Nutritional Facts:

- Calories: 49
- Fat: 2 g
- Carbohydrates: 4 g
- Protein: 3 g

Perfect Air Fryer Salmon

Serves: 2

Cook Time: 8 minutes

Ingredients

- 2 wild caught salmon fillets with comparable thickness (mine were 1-1/12-inches thick)
- 2 tsp avocado oil or olive oil
- 2 tsp paprika
- Generously seasoned with salt and coarse black pepper
- Lemon wedges

Directions

1. Remove any bones from your salmon (if necessary) and let fish sit on the counter for an hour. Rub each fillet with olive oil and season with paprika, salt, and pepper.
2. Place fillets in the basket of the air fryer. Set air fryer at 390 degrees for 7 minutes for 1- ½-inch fillets.
3. When timer goes off, open basket and check fillets with a fork to make sure they are done to your desired cook.

Nutritional Facts:

- Calories: 288
- Fat: 19 g
- Carbohydrates: 2 g
- Protein: 28 g

Parmesan Buttermilk Chicken Tenders

Serves: 4

Cook Time: 15 minutes

Ingredients

- 2 boneless skinless chicken breasts
- ¾ cup buttermilk
- 1 ½ tsp Worcestershire sauce, divided
- ¾ tsp kosher salt, divided
- ¾ tsp freshly ground black pepper, divided
- ½ tsp smoked paprika, divided
- 2 TBSP butter
- 1 ½ cups panko crumbs

- ¼ cup ground Parmesan cheese
- 2 large eggs
- ½ cup flour
- Honey mustard sauce, barbecue sauce, or ranch dressing for dipping

Directions

1. Preheat the air fryer to 400°F. Place the chicken tenders in the basket, adding in batches so as not to crowd or overlap. Cook for 13-15 minutes, flipping the chicken halfway through so they're crispy on both sides. Repeat with the remaining tenders.
2. Serve with sauces. Can be refrigerated for 3 days. Freeze for up to 2 months and reheat from frozen for 20-25 min at 350°F.

Nutritional Facts:

- Calories: 288
- Fat: 19 g
- Carbohydrates: 2 g
- Protein: 28 g

Roasted Asian Broccoli

Serves: 4

Cook Time: 20 minutes

Ingredients

- 1 lb broccoli, cut into florets
- 1 ½ TBSP peanut oil
- 1 TBSP garlic, minced
- Sea salt, to taste
- 2 TBSP reduced-sodium soy sauce
- 2 tsp honey (or agave)
- 2 tsp sriracha
- 1 tsp rice vinegar

- 1/3 cup roasted salted peanuts
- Fresh lime juice (optional)

Directions

1. In a large bowl, toss together the broccoli, peanut oil, garlic and season with sea salt. Make sure the oil covers all the broccoli florets. I like to use my hands to give each one a quick rub.
2. Spread, the broccoli into the wire basket of your air fryer, in as single of a layer as possible, trying to leave a little bit of space between each floret.
3. Cook at 400° until golden brown and crispy, about 15-20 minutes, stirring halfway.
4. While the broccoli and peanuts cook, mix together the honey, soy sauce, sriracha and rice vinegar in a small, microwave-safe bowl.
5. Once mixed, microwave the mixture for 10-15 seconds until the honey is melted and evenly incorporated.
6. Transfer the cooked broccoli to a bowl and add in the soy sauce mixture. Toss to coat and season to taste with a pinch more salt, if needed.
7. Stir in the peanuts and squeeze lime on top (if desired).
8. DEVOUR!

Nutritional Facts:

- Calories: 154
- Fat: 10 g
- Carbohydrates: 10 g
- Protein: 7 g

Chicken Parmesan in the Air Fryer

Serves: 4

Cook Time: 10 minutes

Ingredients

- 2 approximately 8-oz chicken breasts (each), sliced in half to make 4 thinner cutlets
- 6 TBSP seasoned breadcrumbs (I used whole wheat, you can use gluten-free)
- 2 TBSP grated Parmesan cheese
- 1 TBSP butter, melted (or olive oil)
- 6 TBSP reduced-fat mozzarella cheese
- ½ cup marinara

- Cooking spray

Directions

1. Preheat the air fryer 360° for 3 minutes.
2. Combine breadcrumbs and Parmesan cheese in a bowl. Melt the butter in another bowl.
3. Lightly brush the butter onto the chicken, then dip into breadcrumb mixture.
4. When the air fryer is ready, place 2 pieces in the basket and spray the top with oil.
5. Cook 6 minutes, turn and top each with 1 TBSP sauce and 1 ½ TBSP of shredded mozzarella cheese.
6. Cook 3 more minutes or until cheese is melted.
7. Set aside and keep warm, repeat with the remaining 2 pieces.

Nutritional Facts:

- Calories: 250
- Fat: 10 g
- Carbohydrates: 14 g
- Protein: 30 g

Baked Sweet Potato

Serves: 3

Cook Time: 35 minutes

Ingredients

- 3 sweet potatoes
- 1 TBSP olive oil
- 1-2 tsp kosher salt

Directions

1. Wash your sweet potatoes and then create air holes with a fork in the potatoes.
2. Sprinkle them with the olive oil & salt, then rub evenly on the potatoes.

3. Once the potatoes are coated, place them into the basket for the air fryer and place into the machine.

4. Cook your potatoes at 392° for 35-40 minutes, or until fork tender.

5. Top with your favorites!

Nutritional Facts:

- Calories: 153
- Fat: 4 g
- Carbohydrates: 26 g
- Protein: 2 g

Sriracha-Honey Chicken Wings

Serves: 4

Cook Time: 35 minutes

Ingredients

- 1 lb chicken wings, tips removed and wings cut into individual drummettes and flats.
- ¼ cup honey
- 2 TBSP sriracha sauce
- 1 ½ TBSP soy sauce
- 1 TBSP butter
- Juice of half a lime
- Cilantro, chives, or scallions for garnish

Directions

1. Preheat, the air fryer to 360°. Add the chicken wings to the air fryer basket and cook for 30 minutes, turning the chicken about every 7 minutes with tongs to make sure the wings are evenly browned.
2. While the wings are cooking, add the sauce ingredients to a small saucepan and bring to a boil for about 3 minutes.
3. When the wings are cooked, toss them in a bowl with the sauce until fully coated, sprinkle with the garnish, and serve immediately.

Nutritional Facts:

- Calories: 153
- Fat: 4 g
- Carbohydrates: 26 g
- Protein: 2 g

Chicken Nuggets Recipe

Serves: 4

Cook Time: 10 minutes

Ingredients

- 1 boneless skinless chicken breast
- ¼ tsp salt
- 1/8 tsp black pepper
- ½ cup unsalted butter, melted
- ½ cup breadcrumbs
- 2 TBSP grated Parmesan (optional)

Directions

1. Preheat air fryer to 390° for 4 minutes.

2. Trim any fat from the chicken breast, Slice into ½-inch-thick slices, then each slice into 2 to 3 nuggets. Season chicken pieces with salt and pepper.

3. Place melted butter in a small bowl and breadcrumbs (with Parmesan, if using) in another small bowl.

4. Dip each piece of chicken in butter, then breadcrumbs.

5. Place in a single layer in the air fryer basket. Depending on the size of your air fryer, you may need to bake in two batches or more.

6. Set timer to 8 minutes.

7. When done, check if the internal temperature of chicken nuggets is at least 165°. Remove nuggets from basket with tongs and set onto a plate to cool.

Nutritional Facts:

- Calories: 364
- Fat: 24 g
- Carbohydrates: 15 g
- Protein: 24 g

Mexican Street Corn Recipe

Serves: 4

Cook Time: 15 minutes

Ingredients

- 4 pieces fresh corn on the cob, cleaned
- ¼ cup crumbled cotija cheese or feta cheese
- ¼ tsp chili powder
- ½ tsp seasoning (salt, pepper, and garlic)
- ¼ cup fresh cilantro, chopped
- 1 medium lime, cut into wedges

Directions

1. Place corn into the air fryer basket and cook at 390°F for 10 minutes.

2. Sprinkle corn with cheese and cook at 390°F for 5 more minutes.

3. Remove from air fryer and sprinkle with chili powder, Stone House Seasoning, and cilantro. Serve with lime wedges.

Nutritional Facts:

- Calories: 102
- Fat: 3 g
- Carbohydrates: 17 g
- Protein: 4 g

Shrimp Scampi

Serves: 4

Cook Time: 10 minutes

Ingredients

- 4 TBSP butter
- 1 TBSP lemon juice
- 1 TBSP garlic, minced
- 2 tsp red pepper flakes
- 1 TBSP chopped chives or 1 tsp dried chives
- 1 TBSP basil leaves, minced (plus more for sprinkling), or 1 tsp dried basil
- 2 TBSP chicken stock (or white wine)

- 1 lb defrosted shrimp (21-25 count)

Directions

1. Turn your air fryer to 330°F. Place a 6 x 3 metal pan in it and allow the oven to start heating while you gather your ingredients.
2. Place the butter, garlic, and red pepper flakes into the hot 6-inch pan.
3. Allow it to cook for 2 minutes, stirring once, until the butter has melted. Do not skip this step. This is what infuses garlic into the butter, which is what makes it all taste so good.
4. Open, the air fryer, add all ingredients to the pan in the order listed , stirring gently.
5. Allow shrimp to cook for 5 minutes, stirring once. At this point, the butter should be well-melted and liquid, bathing the shrimp in spiced goodness.
6. Mix very well, remove the 6-inch pan using silicone mitts and let it rest for 1 minute on the counter. You're doing this so that you let the shrimp cook in the residual heat, rather than letting it accidentally overcook and become rubbery.
7. Stir at the end of the minute. The shrimp should be well-cooked at this point.
8. Sprinkle additional fresh basil leaves and enjoy.

Nutritional Facts:

- Calories: 213
- Fat: 13 g
- Carbohydrates: 1 g
- Protein: 24 g

Mozzarella Sticks

Serves: 24

Cook Time: 5 minutes

Ingredients

- 1 (10 oz) package part skim mozzarella string cheese, each stick cut in half
- ¼ cup whole wheat flour
- 1 large egg
- ¼ cup breadcrumbs
- ¼ cup panko
- ½ - 1 tsp onion powder
- ½ - 1 tsp garlic powder

- ½ - 1 tsp salt
- ½ - 1 tsp chili powder
- ½ - 1 tsp smoked paprika
- Marinara sauce, for dipping
- Ranch, for dipping

Directions

1. Place halved cheese sticks into a ziplock baggie and place in freezer until frozen, at least 30 minutes.
2. Place egg into a shallow bowl and whisk until broken up. Set aside.
3. Place breadcrumbs, panko, onion powder, garlic powder, salt, chili powder, and smoked paprika in another shallow bowl and whisk until well-combined. Set aside.
4. Line a rimmed baking sheet with a silicone mat or parchment paper.
5. Place frozen cheese sticks and flour into another ziplock baggie (the one from the freezer will have too many ice chunks) and shake until the cheese sticks are fully coated in the flour.
6. Discard excess flour.
7. Dunk one cheese stick in egg until fully coated and then in panko mixture until fully coated.

8. Place on lined baking sheet and repeat with remaining cheese sticks.

9. Place baking sheet in freezer until all the cheese sticks have re-frozen, at least an hour.

10. Press **ON** on the air fryer.

11. Then press **PRE-HEAT**. Set the temperature to 370°F and set the timer to 5 minutes.

12. Press **START**.

13. The air fryer will beep at you when it's finished preheating.

14. Open up the air fryer and spray the basket with cooking spray.

15. Place in the mozzarella sticks, work with about 6 at a time, so you don't overcrowd them.

16. Close the air fryer. It will beep at you when it's finished cooking.

17. Repeat with as many mozzarella sticks as you'd like. Store uncooked leftovers in the freezer!

18. Serve with dipping sauces and enjoy!

Nutritional Facts:

- Calories: 48
- Fat: 2 g
- Carbohydrates: 2 g
- Protein: 3 g

Spicy Chicken Empanadas

Serves: 4

Cook Time: 15 minutes

Ingredients

- 1 box of refrigerated pie crust
- 2 rolls
- 1 cup shredded rotisserie chicken
- ½ cup shredded cheddar cheese
- ¼ cup green onion/scallions, chopped
- ½ cup cilantro, chopped
- 2 chopped Jalapeno, seeds and membrane removed
- ½ tsp garlic powder

- ½ tsp ground cumin
- 2 tsp hot sauce
- Salt and pepper, to taste
- Egg wash (1 egg whisked with 1 TBSP water)

CILANTRO-SCALLION DIPPING SAUCE
- ½ cup sour cream
- 1 tsp green onion/scallion, chopped
- ½ cup cilantro, chopped
- ¼ tsp cayenne pepper
- ¼ tsp smoked Paprika
- Salt, to taste

Directions
1. In a large bowl, combine shredded chicken, cheddar cheese, chopped green onions, jalapeno and cilantro, garlic powder, ground cumin, hot sauce, and salt and pepper. Mix well.
2. Unroll the pie dough onto a well-floured surface. Using, a 5-inch circular cookie cutter, cut out as many circles as possible. Using, a rolling-pin, roll out the scraps and continue to cut out circles until the dough runs out. We got 10 circles from 1 pie dough.

3. Repeat the same with the other pie dough. Spoon about 1 TBSP of the spicy chicken filling into middle of dough. Moisten edges with egg wash.

4. Fold the dough in half over the filling, forming a half circle, then use the fingers to gently press and seal the edges. Use a fork to crimp the edges together.

5. Brush each empanadas with the egg wash.

6. Air fry the empanadas at 400°F for 10 minutes.

7. Serve hot with cilantro-scallion dipping sauce.

Nutritional Facts:

- Calories: 175
- Fat: 10 g
- Carbohydrates: 12 g
- Protein: 6 g

Chicken Fried Rice

Serves: 4

Cook Time: 20 minutes

Ingredients

- 3 cups cooked white rice, cold
- 1 cup cooked chicken, diced
- 1 cup frozen peas and carrots
- 6 TBSP soy sauce
- 1 TBSP vegetable oil
- ½ cup onion, diced

Directions

1. Place the cold cooked white rice into the mixing bowl.
2. Add the vegetable oil and the soy sauce and mix thoroughly.
3. Add the frozen peas & carrots, the diced onion, and the diced chicken and mix thoroughly.
4. Pour the rice mixture into the nonstick pan (if using the aluminum pan then spray it with nonstick cooking spray first).
5. Place the pan into the air fryer.
6. Set the air fryer to 360° with a 20-minute cook time.
7. Once the timer goes off, remove the pan from the air fryer.
8. Serve with your favorite meat or just grab a bowl and enjoy!

Nutritional Facts:

- Calories: 420
- Fat: 5 g
- Carbohydrates: 80 g
- Protein: 16 g

Garlic Baked Potatoes

Serves: 4

Cook Time: 35 minutes

Ingredients

- 3 Idaho or russet baking potatoes
- 1-2 TBSP olive oil
- 1 TBSP salt
- 1 TBSP garlic
- 1 tsp parsley

Directions

1. Wash your potatoes and then create air holes with a fork in the potatoes.

2. Sprinkle them with the olive oil and seasonings, then rub the seasoning evenly on the potatoes.

3. Once the potatoes are coated, place them into the basket for the air fryer and place into the machine.

4. Cook your potatoes at 392° for 35-40 minutes or until fork tender.

5. Top with your favorites. We love fresh parsley and sour cream!

Nutritional Facts:

- Calories: 213
- Fat: 4 g
- Carbohydrates: 40 g
- Protein: 4 g

3-Ingredient Fried Catfish

Serves: 4

Cook Time: 60 minutes

Ingredients

- 4 catfish fillets
- ¼ cup seasoned fish fry (I used Louisiana)
- 1 TBSP olive oil
- 1 TBSP parsley, chopped (optional)

Directions

1. Preheat air fryer to 400°.
2. Rinse the catfish and pat dry.

3. Pour the fish fry seasoning in a large Ziploc bag.

4. Add the catfish to the bag, one at a time. Seal the bag and shake. Ensure the entire filet is coated with seasoning.

5. Spray olive oil on the top of each filet.

6. Place the filet in the air fryer basket (due to the size of my fillets, I cooked each one at a time). Close and cook for 10 minutes.

7. Flip the fish. Cook for an additional 10 minutes.

8. Flip the fish.

9. Cook for an additional 2-3 minutes or until desired crispness.

10. Top with parsley.

Nutritional Facts:

- Calories: 208
- Fat: 9 g
- Carbohydrates: 8 g
- Protein: 17 g

Bang Bang Shrimp

Serves: 4

Cook Time: 20 minutes

Ingredients

- 1 lb raw shrimp, peeled and deveined
- 1 egg white (3 TBSP)
- ½ cup all-purpose flour
- 3/4 cup panko bread crumbs
- 1 tsp paprika
- McCormick's Grill Mates Montreal Chicken Seasoning, to taste
- Salt and pepper, to taste
- Cooking spray

BANG BANG SAUCE

- 1/3 cup plain, non-fat Greek yogurt
- 2 TBSP sriracha
- ¼ cup sweet chili sauce

Directions

1. Preheat air fryer to 400°.
2. Season the shrimp with the seasonings.
3. Place the flour, egg whites, and panko bread crumbs in three separate bowls.
4. Create a cooking station. Dip the shrimp in the flour, then the egg whites, and the panko bread crumbs last.
5. When dipping the shrimp in the egg whites, you do not need to submerge the shrimp. Do a light dab so that most of the flour stays on the shrimp. You want the egg white to adhere to the panko crumbs.
6. Spray the shrimp with cooking spray. Do not spray directly on the shrimp. The panko will go flying. Keep a nice distance.
7. Add the shrimp to the air fryer basket. Cook for 4 minutes. Open the basket and flip the shrimp to the other side. Cook for an additional 4 minutes or until crisp.

BANG BANG SAUCE

8. Combine, all of the ingredients, in a small bowl, mix thoroughly.

Nutritional Facts:

- Calories: 208
- Fat: 9 g
- Carbohydrates: 8 g
- Protein: 17 g

Greek Spinach and Turkey Pie

Serves: 4

Cook Time: 20 minutes

Ingredients

- Leftover turkey (brown meat), shredded
- Filo pastry
- 2 large eggs
- 1 small egg, reserved for pastry brushing
- 200 g spinach
- 1 large onion
- 250 g cream cheese
- 100 g feta cheese, chopped into small cubes
- 1 tsp basil
- 1 TBSP oregano

- 1 TBSP thyme
- Salt and pepper, to taste

Directions

1. Get your leftover vegetables out of the fridge and season well with salt and pepper.
2. Place your vegetables inside a teatowel or pillowcase and ring out any excess moisture. Place them in a mixing bowl with your seasoning and your feta cheese.
3. Mix in your egg and your soft cheese until you have a lovely creamy mixture.
4. Line a dish with filo pastry and add your mixture to it so that it is ¾ full. Cover with the remainder of the pastry and then brush with beaten egg.
5. Air fry for 20 minutes on 180°C.

Nutritional Facts:

- Calories: 385
- Fat: 32 g
- Carbohydrates: 9 g
- Protein: 17 g

Potato Latke Bites

Serves: 14

Cook Time: 10 minutes

Ingredients

- 4 large potatoes
- 1 large yellow/brown onion
- 4 large eggs
- 1/3 cup Matzo Meal
- 1 TBSP potato starch
- 2 tsp kosher salt
- ½ tsp freshly ground black pepper
- ½ tsp baking powder (optional)
- Grapeseed oil

Directions

1. Wash potatoes and peel. Run through food processor to grate and then place in a bowl with cool water. Set aside.

2. Rinse out food processor and grate onions. Place onion in tea towel or paper towel and squeeze out all liquid.

3. In a medium mixing bowl, whisk together eggs. Add salt, pepper, Matzo Meal, potato starch, baking powder (if using) and grated onions.

4. Drain water from potatoes and save the starch left in the bowl. Squeeze out all water from potatoes and add to onion mixture. Scoop out the starch from the potato bowl and add to Latkes mixture.

5. Generously spray silicone trays with oil. Fill each well with the Latkes mixture and generously spray with oil.

6. Air fry at 350° for 6 minutes. Remove air fryer basket and pop out bites into air fryer. Spray generously and cook for 4 additional minutes at 400°. Serve with applesauce and sour cream.

Nutritional Facts:

- Calories: 62
- Fat: 3 g
- Carbohydrates: 6 g
- Protein: 1 g

Jalapeño Poppers

Serves: 10

Cook Time: 10 minutes

Ingredients

- 10 jalapeno peppers, halved and de-seeded
- 8 oz cream cheese (I used a dairy-free cream cheese)
- ¼ cup fresh parsley
- ¾ cup gluten-free tortilla or bread crumbs

Directions

1. Mix together half of the crumbs and cream cheese. Once combined, add in the parsley.
2. Stuff each pepper with this mixture.
3. Gently press the tops of the peppers into the remaining ¼ cup of crumbs to create the top coating.
4. Cook in an air fryer at 370°F for 6-8 minutes OR in a conventional oven at 375°F for 20 minutes.
5. Let cool and ENJOY!

Nutritional Facts:

- Calories: 104
- Fat: 8 g
- Carbohydrates: 4 g
- Protein: 5 g

Flourless Fried Chicken

Serves: 4

Cook Time: 25 minutes

Ingredients

- 8 chicken drumsticks
- 50 g gluten-free oats
- 50 g cauliflower
- 1 large egg, beaten
- 50 ml coconut milk
- 2 TBSP thyme
- 2 TBSP oregano
- 2 TBSP mustard powder
- 1 tsp cayenne pepper
- Salt and pepper, to taste

Directions

1. Preheat your air fryer to 180°C.

2. On your chopping board, lay out your chicken and sprinkle all sides with salt and pepper. After you have done this, rub coconut milk into them.

3. Place everything else (apart from the egg) into your blender a bit at a time. Blend on the low blend feature until it is like smooth breadcrumbs.

4. Place the breadcrumb mixture into a bowl and the egg into another bowl.

5. Then for each piece of chicken, dip it into the breadcrumbs, then into the egg, and then back into the breadcrumbs.

6. Place them onto a baking mat inside your air fryer and cook for 20 minutes with 4 chicken pieces in your air fryer so that it is not overcrowded.

7. Cook at 180°C and then, after you've done the 20 minutes, give it another 5 minutes at 200°C so that it can get nice and crispy.

8. Serve.

Nutritional Facts:

- Calories: 361
- Fat: 20 g
- Carbohydrates: 14 g
- Protein: 32 g

Ranch Kale Chips

Serves: 2

Cook Time: 5 minutes

Ingredients

- 2 TBSP olive oil
- 4 cups loosely-packed kale, stemmed
- 2 tsp ranch seasoning
- 1 TBSP nutritional yeast flakes
- ¼ tsp salt

Directions

1. Toss the oil, kale pieces, ranch seasoning, and
   nutritional yeast together in a medium-sized bowl,

then dump the coated kale into the basket of your air fryer.

2. Cook on 370° for 4-5 minutes (do not preheat), shaking after 2 minutes. Eat immediately.

Nutritional Facts:

- Calories: 150
- Fat: 15 g
- Carbohydrates: 3 g
- Protein: 2 g

Breakfast Pockets

Serves: 2

Cook Time: 15 minutes

Ingredients

- 1 box puff pastry sheets
- 5 eggs
- ½ cup sausage crumbles, cooked
- ½ cup bacon, cooked
- ½ cup cheddar cheese, shredded

Directions

1. Cook eggs as regular scrambled eggs. Add meat to the egg mixture while you cook, if desired.

2. Spread out puff pastry sheets on a cutting board and cut out rectangles with a cookie cutter or knife, making sure they are all uniform so they will fit nicely together.

3. Spoon preferred egg, meat, and cheese combos onto half of the pastry rectangles.

4. Place a pastry rectangle on top of the mixture and press edges together with a fork to seal.

5. Spray with spray oil if you desire a shiny, smooth pastry, but it really is optional.

6. Place breakfast pockets in the air fryer basket and cook for 8-10 minutes at 370°.

7. Watch carefully and check every 2-3 minutes for desired cook.

Nutritional Facts:

- Calories: 250
- Fat: 15 g
- Carbohydrates: 15 g
- Protein: 8 g

Crispy Steak Fries

Serves: 6

Cook Time: 20 minutes

Ingredients

- 2 russet potatoes, washed
- 1 TBSP olive oil
- 1 TBSP Pappy's Seasoning (optional)
- 2 TBSP granulated garlic
- ¼ cup shredded Parmesan cheese (you can use grated too)
- ¼ tsp salt
- ¼ tsp pepper

Directions

1. Cut potatoes into wedges and place in a large bowl.
2. Drizzle olive oil over potatoes and add seasonings.
3. Toss to combine and coat.
4. Transfer to air fryer basket and insert into the machine.
5. Set the air fryer to 400° and cook for 20 minutes (stirring halfway through)
6. Serve with ranch dressing or ketchup

Nutritional Facts:

- Calories: 278
- Fat: 10 g
- Carbohydrates: 40 g
- Protein: 8 g

Roasted Broccoli in Spicy Yogurt Marinade

Serves: 2

Cook Time: 10 minutes

Ingredients
- 500 g broccoli

MARINADE
- 2 TBSP yogurt
- 1 TBSP chickpea flour
- ¼ tsp turmeric powder
- ½ tsp salt
- ½ tsp red chilli powder
- ¼ tsp Chaat Masala

Directions

1. To prepare crispy roasted broccoli, cut the broccoli into small florets. Soak in a bowl of water with 2 tsp salt for 30 minutes to remove any impurities or worms.

2. Remove the broccoli florets from the water. Drain well and wipe thoroughly using a kitchen towel to absorb all the moisture.

3. In a bowl, mix together all the ingredients for the marinade.

4. Toss the broccoli florets in this marinade. Cover and keep aside in the refrigerator for 15 minutes.

5. When the broccoli is marinated, preheat the air fryer at 200°C. Open the basket of the air fryer and place the marinated florets inside. Push the basket back in, and turn the time dial to 10 minutes.

6. Give the basket a shake once midway and then check after 10 minutes if golden and crisp. If not, keep for another 2-3 minutes. Eat them hot!

Nutritional Facts:

- Calories: 96
- Fat: 2 g
- Carbohydrates: 17 g
- Protein: 8 g

Sugar-Dusted Doughnuts

Serves: 8

Cook Time: 10 minutes

Ingredients

- 8 biscuits (you can use any generic brand)
- 3 TBSP butter, melted
- 1/3 cup granulated sugar
- ½ to 1 tsp cinnamon (adjust to your taste)
- 4 TBSP dark brown sugar (try to remove or break up any clumps)
- Pinch of Allspice

Directions

1. Combine sugar, cinnamon, brown sugar, and Allspice in a small (cereal or soup-sized) bowl and set aside.

2. Remove biscuits from can (do not flatten) and use a 1-inch circle biscuit cutter to cut the holes out of the center of each biscuit.

3. Air fry the donuts at 350°F for 5 minutes (I fried 4 at a time), and air fry the holes at 350°F for just 3 minutes (I fried all 8 holes at once).

4. As each batch of donuts and holes comes out of the fryer, use a pastry brush to paint butter over the entire surface of each donut and hole.

5. After each donut and hole is painted with butter, drop into the bowl with the sugar mixture and coat completely with the mixture. Gently shake off excess.

6. Serve donuts and holes warm.

Nutritional Facts:

- Calories: 210
- Fat: 8 g
- Carbohydrates: 30 g
- Protein: 3 g

Lemon Pepper Chicken

Serves: 1

Cook Time: 15 minutes

Ingredients

- 1 chicken breast
- 2 lemons, rind, and juice
- 1 TBSP chicken seasoning
- 1 tsp garlic puree
- Handful of black peppercorns
- Salt and pepper, to taste

Directions

1. Preheat the air fryer to 180°C.

2. Set up your work station. Place a large sheet of silver foil on the work top and add to it all the seasonings and the lemon rinds.

3. Lay out your chicken breasts onto a chopping board and trim off any fatty bits or any little bones that are still there. Then season each side with salt and pepper. Rub the chicken seasoning onto both sides so that it is a slightly different color.

4. Place it in the silver foil sheet and rub it well so that it is fully seasoned.

5. Then seal it up very tight so that it can't breathe, as this will help get the flavor into it.

6. Then give it a slap with a rolling pin so that it will flatten it out and release more flavor.

7. Place it in the air fryer for 15 minutes and check to see if it is fully cooked in the middle before serving.

8. Serve.

Nutritional Facts:

- Calories: 140
- Fat: 2 g
- Carbohydrates: 24 g
- Protein: 13 g

Buffalo Cauliflower

Serves: 4

Cook Time: 15 minutes

Ingredients

CAULIFLOWER

- 4 cups cauliflower florets – Each one should be approximately the size of two baby carrots, if you put the baby carrots side-by-side.
- 1 cup panko breadcrumbs mixed with 1 tsp sea salt

BUFFALO COATING

- ¼ cup melted vegan butter – ¼ cup after melting
- ¼ cup Frank's Red Hot Buffalo Sauce

DIPPING

- Vegan mayo – Cashew Ranch, or your favorite creamy salad dressing

Directions

1. Melt the vegan butter in a mug in the microwave, then whisk in the buffalo sauce.

2. Holding by the stem, dip each floret in the butter/buffalo mixture, getting most of the floret coated in sauce. It's fine if a bit of the stem doesn't get saucy. Hold the floret over the mug until it pretty much stops dripping. A few drips are okay, but if it's raining sauce, your panko is going to get clumpy and stop sticking as well.

3. Dredge the dipped floret in the panko/salt mixture, coating as much as you like, then place in the air fryer. No need to worry about a single layer. Just drop it in there.

4. Air fry at 350°F (do not preheat) for 14-17 minutes, shaking a few times, and checking their progress when

you shake. Your cauliflower is done when the florets are a little bit browned.

5. Serve with your dipping sauce of choice.

Nutritional Facts:

- Calories: 97
- Fat: 8 g
- Carbohydrates: 5 g
- Protein: 2 g

Crunchy Basil Croutons

Serves: 8

Cook Time: 5 minutes

Ingredients

- 2 heaping cups cubed baguette (or your preferred bread), cut in 1-inch pieces
- 2 tsp extra virgin olive oil
- 2 tsp lemon juice
- ½ tsp dried oregano
- ½ tsp dried basil
- ½ tsp granulated garlic

- Pinch of salt and pepper

Directions

1. Put cubed baguette into a large mixing bowl. Evenly drizzle extra virgin olive oil and lemon juice across the bread. Then sprinkle on dried oregano, dried basil, garlic granules, salt, and pepper.
2. Use your hands to toss the cubed bread, getting everything evenly coated, and making sure the spices are on the bread instead of stuck on the sides of the bowl.
3. Put the bread into the air fryer. Cook at 400° for 5 minutes, stopping once or twice to shake the basket.
4. Serve on top of your favorite salad.

Nutritional Facts:

- Calories: 30
- Fat: 1 g
- Carbohydrates: 4 g
- Protein: 0 g

Tuna Patties

Serves: 2

Cook Time: 15 minutes

Ingredients

- 2 cans tuna, packed in water
- 1 ½ TBSP almond flour
- 1 ½ TBSP mayo
- 1 tsp dried dill
- 1 tsp garlic powder
- ½ tsp onion powder
- Pinch of salt and pepper
- Juice of half a lemon

Directions

1. Combine all ingredients in a bowl and mix well
2. Tuna should still be wet, but able to form into patties – add an additional TBSP of almond flour if it's not dry enough to form
3. Form into 4 patties
4. Heat to 400°F.
5. Place patties in a single layer in the basket and cook for 10 minutes. Add an additional 3 minutes if you'd like them crispier

Nutritional Facts:

- Calories: 130
- Fat: 5 g
- Carbohydrates: 5 g
- Protein: 15 g

Buffalo Wings

Serves: 4

Cook Time: 30 minutes

Ingredients
- 2 lbs chicken wings or drummies
- ½ cup Frank's Hot Sauce
- ½ cup ghee
- ½ tsp salt
- ½ tsp pepper
- 2 TBSP olive oil (if cooking in the oven)

Directions
1. Set the air fryer to 375°F.

2. Season chicken wings with salt and pepper and place into the air fryer basket.

3. Cook the wings for 20 minutes, flipping with tongs after 10 minutes.

4. When time is up, flip one last time and increase the temperature to 400°F.

5. Cook an additional 8 minutes until skin is crispy and golden.

6. When there's about a minute left on the timer, heat hot sauce and ghee in a small dish in the microwave for 45 seconds, or until ghee is melted.

7. Stir together to combine.

8. Remove wings from air fryer and place in a bowl or serving dish.

9. Toss with buffalo sauce and enjoy!

Nutritional Facts:

- Calories: 490
- Fat: 47 g
- Carbohydrates: 0 g
- Protein: 16 g

Artichoke Hearts

Serves: 4

Cook Time: 15 minutes

Ingredients
- 1 bag of frozen artichoke hearts (preservative-free)
- 1 cup arrowroot flour (gluten-free and easily digestible)
- 1-2 eggs
- 1 TBSP Organic Herb de Provence
- Clean oil or ghee for coating air fryer basket

Directions
1. Mix 1 cup of arrowroot flour in a bowl with the Herb de Provence and incorporate.

2. In a separate bowl, whisk 1-2 eggs to create an egg wash.

3. Dip each artichoke in the egg mixture and transfer to flour mixture for coating (be sure to keep the flour mix from your hands out of the egg wash).

4. Coat basket of air fryer with ghee or a clean oil to prevent sticking.

5. Set air fryer on the **CHIPS** feature for 15 minutes.

6. Using tongs, carefully flip the artichokes halfway.

Nutritional Facts:

- Calories: 120
- Fat: 5 g
- Carbohydrates: 14 g
- Protein: 2 g

Plantain Chips

Serves: 1

Cook Time: 15 minutes

Ingredients

- 1 each green plantain
- 1 tsp canola oil or canola cooking spray
- ½ tsp sea salt, or to taste

Directions

1. Peel, the plantains, cut them in half and slice into very thin coins or strips. NOTE: Use a mandolin slicer if you want consistent, ultra-thin slices.

2. Coat the fryer basket with ½ tsp of canola oil and lay the plantain slices along the bottom. Brush the remaining canola oil on top of the slices. Season with sea salt, to taste.

3. Air fry your plantain chips at 350°F for 15-20 minutes depending on the thickness of your slices. Be sure to shake your basket once or twice during the air frying process to be sure they are evenly cooked. Watch them closely after about 10 minutes to prevent burning. If you've sliced them unevenly, you may need to pick a few out each time you check in. NOTE: If your plantains start to stick to the bottom, just lift them off with a pair of tongs and give the basket a good shake.

4. Nosh on your air fryer plantain chips right out of the fryer, or serve with your favorite condiment. Enjoy!

Nutritional Facts:

- Calories: 109
- Fat: 1 g
- Carbohydrates: 28 g
- Protein: 2 g

Dill Pickle Chips

Serves: 2

Cook Time: 10 minutes

Ingredients

- 1 jar dill pickles
- 200 g gluten-free oats
- 1 tsp basil
- Salt and pepper, to taste

Directions

1. Chop your dill pickles into thirds and don't drain the pickle juice from them.

2. In a blender, add gluten-free oats, salt, pepper, and basil and blend until it resembles breadcrumbs. Place it into a large bowl.

3. Place the dill pickles into the dry ingredients and make sure it is well-coated.

4. Place the dill pickles into the air fryer and cook for 4 minutes on each side at 200°C/400°F.

5. Serve while still warm.

Nutritional Facts:

- Calories: 382
- Fat: 6 g
- Carbohydrates: 70 g
- Protein: 12 g

Marinated Steak

Serves: 2

Cook Time: 10 minutes

Ingredients

- 2 Butcher Box New York Strip Steaks (mine were about 6-8 oz each). You can use any cut of steak
- 1 TBSP low-sodium soy sauce (this is used to provide liquid to marinate the meat and make it juicy)
- 1 tsp liquid smoke, or a cap full
- 1 TBSP McCormick's Grill Mates Montreal Steak Seasoning or Steak Rub (or season to taste) See recipe notes for instructions on how to create your own steak rub
- ½ TBSP unsweetened cocoa powder

- Salt and pepper, to taste
- Melted butter (optional)

Directions

1. Drizzle the Butcher Box Steak with the soy sauce and liquid smoke. You can do this inside Ziploc bags.
2. Season the steak with the seasonings.
3. Refrigerate for at least a couple of hours, preferably overnight.
4. Place the steak in the air fryer. I did not use any oil. Cook two steaks at a time (if air fryer is standard size). You can use an accessory grill pan, a layer rack, or the standard air fryer basket.
5. Cook for 5 minutes on 375°. After 5 minutes, open the air fryer and examine your steak. Cook time will vary depending on your desired cook. Check the inside of the steak to determine if it has finished cooking. You can stick a knife or fork in the center to review the level of pink. You can also use a meat thermometer and cook to 125° F for rare, 135° F for medium-rare, 145° F for medium, 155° F for medium-well, and 160° F for well-done.
6. For medium steak, at 5 minutes, I flipped my steak and cooked for an additional 2 minutes, 7 minutes cook time total using the Power Air Fryer. Each air

fryer brand is different and will cook at different speeds. I also have the Black + Decker Air Fryer, and 5 minutes at 370° was enough time to produce medium-well steak. At 7 minutes, the steak was near well-done. Examine your steak and do what works best for you.

7. Remove the steak from the air fryer and drizzle with melted butter.

Nutritional Facts:

- Calories: 480
- Fat: 28 g
- Carbohydrates: 2 g
- Protein: 50 g

Kofta Kababs

Serves: 4

Cook Time: 10 minutes

Ingredients

- 1 TBSP oil
- 1 lb lean ground beef
- ¼ cup parsley, chopped
- 1 TBSP garlic, minced
- 2 TBSP kofta kabab spice mix
- 1 tsp salt

Directions

1. Using, a stand mixer, blend together all ingredients. If you have time, let the mixture sit in the fridge for 30

minutes. You can also mix it up and set aside for a day, or two until you're ready to make the kababs

2. Although I tried this with and without skewers, it really makes no difference to the final product. Since it's a lot easier to simply shape the kababs by hand, divide the meat into four and make four long sausage shapes (or Pokémon shape, or whatever you want).

3. Place the kababs in your air fryer and cook at 370°F for 10 minutes.

4. Check with a meat thermometer to ensure that the kababs have an internal temperature of 145°F.

5. Sprinkle with additional parsley for garnishing and serve with tzatziki, a cucumber tomato salad, and pita bread.

Nutritional Facts:

- Calories: 280
- Fat: 20 g
- Carbohydrates: 2 g
- Protein: 21 g

Air Fryer Whole Chicken

Serves: 6

Cook Time: 45 minutes

Ingredients

- 1 whole chicken
- 1 TBSP dry rub
- Salt (optional)
- Calorie-controlled cooking spray or olive oil

Directions

1. Preheat the air fryer to 180°C / 350°F.

2. Pat chicken dry. Rub in the dry rub and sprinkle salt if desired.

3. Spray air fryer with cooking spray.

4. Add chicken in and cook for 30 mins on one side.

5. Then flip and cook for 15-30 mins on other side, depending on the size of your bird.

6. It is important to check that the internal temperature of the chicken is 75°C (165°F) before serving.

Nutritional Facts:

- Calories: 412
- Fat: 28 g
- Carbohydrates: 2 g
- Protein: 35 g

Coconut Shrimp

Serves: 12

Cook Time: 15 minutes

Ingredients

- 12 wild XL shrimp
- 1/3 cup cassava flour
- 2 large eggs, beaten
- ½ cup unsweetened shredded coconut
- 1 lime wedge
- 1 TBSP extra virgin olive oil, for brushing the basket

TROPICAL DIPPING SAUCE

- 4 tsp coconut aminos
- 1 cup pineapple juice
- 1 tsp raw honey
- ¼ tsp ginger powder
- ½ tsp tapioca starch

Directions

1. Wash the shrimp and devein them. Make small slits in the belly of the shrimps, so they don't curl when cooked. Place cassava flour on a plate, the eggs in a shallow bowl and the shredded coconut on another plate. Dredge shrimp in the flour, dip in the egg, and roll and coat with the shredded coconut. Refrigerate for 30 minutes.

2. Preheat the air fryer to 360°F.

3. Brush the basket with extra virgin olive oil. Place 6 shrimp in the basket, in a single layer and set the timer for 7 minutes.

4. Meanwhile, in a small saucepan, bring the pineapple juice to a boil and then simmer on low heat, until it's reduced to half. Add the rest of the ingredients and stir well. Take the pan off the heat and set aside.

5. When the timer goes off, take the shrimp out, place them on a plate, and cover. Put, the rest of the shrimp,

in the basket and cook for 7 minutes. When the timer goes off, squeeze some lime juice on the shrimp, and serve immediately with the Tropical Dipping Sauce.

Nutritional Facts:

- Calories: 236
- Fat: 9 g
- Carbohydrates: 27 g
- Protein: 13 g

Fish and Chips

Serves: 4

Cook Time: 15 minutes

Ingredients

- 1 ¼ lb cod
- 2 large eggs
- 1 cup almond flour
- 1 TBSP dried parsley
- ½ tsp garlic powder
- ½ tsp onion powder
- ¼ tsp salt

- 1 TBSP arrowroot powder (organic cornstarch works too)

Directions

1. In a medium mixing bowl, beat the eggs with a whisk until well-combined.
2. In a separate, medium mixing bowl, mix together the almond flour, parsley, garlic powder, onion powder, salt, and arrowroot powder (or cornstarch). Combine thoroughly.
3. Dip the fish pieces into the egg and then roll in the breading, making sure to cover each part of the fish.
4. Place the fish pieces in a single layer in the basket of the air fryer. Set to 350° for 7 minutes. When done, flip the pieces of fish in the basket and repeat for another 7 minutes.

Nutritional Facts:

- Calories: 340
- Fat: 17 g
- Carbohydrates: 12 g
- Protein: 35 g

Salmon Cakes

Serves: 6

Cook Time: 8 minutes

Ingredients
- 14 oz (400 g) canned salmon
- 3 TBSP cilantro (coriander), chopped
- 3 green onions (spring onions), finely minced
- 1 tsp smoked paprika
- 1 egg
- Salt, to taste

Directions
1. Preheat air fryer to 360°F/180°C.

2. Open salmon, drain, and remove bones (you can leave in if you prefer; I actually like the bones). If using fresh salmon, remove bones and mince by hand.

3. Add all ingredients to a bowl and combine.

4. Form 6 patties, making sure they are the same size.

5. Add patties to the air fryer basket and lightly spray with no-calorie cooking spray.

6. Cook for 6-8 mins, turning the patties over halfway through the cook time.

Nutritional Facts:

- Calories: 104
- Fat: 4 g
- Carbohydrates: 2 g
- Protein: 16 g

Crispy Air Fryer Fish Fillets

Serves: 8

Cook Time: 15 minutes

Ingredients

- 8 (800 g) fish fillets
- 1 TBSP olive oil
- 1 cup 50 g bread crumbs
- ½ tsp paprika
- ¼ tsp dried chili powder
- ¼ tsp ground black pepper

- ¼ tsp garlic powder
- ¼ tsp onion powder
- ½ tsp salt

Directions

1. If using frozen fish fillets, defrost them. Drizzle with olive oil, and mix the fish to make sure that it's well-coated with oil.
2. In a shallow dish, mix the bread crumbs with paprika, chili powder, black pepper, garlic powder, onion powder, and salt.
3. Coat each fish fillet in bread crumbs, and transfer to your air fryer basket.
4. Cook in the air fryer at 390°F or 200°C for 12-15 minutes. After the first 8-10 minutes, open the air fryer and flip the fish fillets on the other side, then continue cooking.

Nutritional Facts:

- Calories: 153
- Fat: 4 g
- Carbohydrates: 11 g
- Protein: 21 g

Lemon Garlic Shrimp

Serves: 2

Cook Time: 15 minutes

Ingredients

- 1 lb raw shrimp, peeled and deveined
- Vegetable oil or spray, to coat shrimp
- ¼ tsp garlic powder
- Salt, to taste
- Black pepper, to taste
- Lemon wedges
- Parsley, minced; and/or chili flakes (optional)

Directions

1. In a bowl, toss the shrimp with the oil. Add garlic powder, salt, and pepper and toss to evenly coat the shrimp.

2. Add shrimp to air fryer basket in a single layer.

3. Air fry at 400°F for about 10-14 minutes, gently shaking and flipping halfway, depending on size of shrimp (about 4 minutes for smaller shrimp, 6 minutes for larger shrimp).

4. Transfer shrimp to bowl, squeeze lemon juice on top. Sprinkle parsley and/or chili flakes and serve hot.

Nutritional Facts:

- Calories: 153
- Fat: 4 g
- Carbohydrates: 11 g
- Protein: 21 g

Sweet Potato Hash Browns

Serves: 4

Cook Time: 20 minutes

Ingredients

- 4 sweet potatoes, peeled
- 2 garlic cloves, minced
- 1 tsp cinnamon
- 1 tsp paprika
- Salt and pepper, to taste
- 2 tsp olive oil

Directions

1. Grate the sweet potatoes using the largest holes of a cheese grater.

2. Place the sweet potatoes in a bowl of cold water. Allow the sweet potatoes to soak for 20-25 minutes. Soaking the sweet potatoes in cold water will help remove the starch from the potatoes. This makes them crunchy.

3. Drain the water from the potatoes and dry them completely using a paper towel.

4. Place the potatoes in a dry bowl. Add the olive oil, garlic, paprika, and salt and pepper to taste. Stir to combine the ingredients.

5. Add the potatoes to the air fryer.

6. Cook for ten minutes on 400°

7. Open the air fryer and shake the potatoes. Cook for an additional ten minutes.

8. Cool before serving.

Nutritional Facts:

- Calories: 153
- Fat: 4 g
- Carbohydrates: 11 g
- Protein: 21 g

Air Fried Asparagus

Serves: 4

Cook Time: 10 minutes

Ingredients

- 2 cups (200 g) fresh asparagus with the ends trimmed (about 2 inches)
- 1 TBSP olive oil spray
- Salt and ground black pepper, to taste
- Nutritional yeast (optional)

IF MAKING WITH MUSHROOMS

- 2/3 cup (50 g) mushrooms, sliced into quarters

- 1/8 cup (20 g) almonds, soaked in warm water for at least 15 minutes
- 1 tsp rosemary, chopped

Directions

1. Start by washing and trimming the ends of the asparagus (about 2 inches just to get rid off the woody part).
2. Spray with olive oil, and sprinkle with salt and ground black pepper. If using mushrooms, add the chopped mushrooms as well.
3. Cook in the air fryer basket for 8 minutes at 390°F (200°c). When ready, serve. If you're making asparagus with mushrooms, then arrange the asparagus and mushrooms on a plate, top with chopped almonds and rosemary.

Nutritional Facts:

- Calories: 63
- Fat: 6 g
- Carbohydrates: 1 g
- Protein: 1 g

Pumpkin French Fries

Serves: 2

Cook Time: 15 minutes

Ingredients
- 250 g pumpkin
- 1 tsp thyme
- 1 TBSP mustard
- Salt and pepper, to taste
- Whole 30 Tomato Ketchup (optional)

Directions
1. Peel, the pumpkin, remove the seeds, and slice into French fries.
2. Place them in the air fryer at 200°C for 15 minutes.

3. Halfway through, shake and season with the thyme, mustard, and salt and pepper.
4. Serve hot with tomato ketchup.

Nutritional Facts:
- Calories: 97
- Fat: 4 g
- Carbohydrates: 10 g
- Protein: 4 g

Mini Blueberry Muffins

Serves: 2

Cook Time: 10 minutes

Ingredients

- 1 cup frozen blueberries
- 1 cup cassava flour, or your favorite gluten-free flour
- 1/3 cup coconut sugar
- ½ tsp salt
- 2 tsp baking powder
- ¼ cup unsweetened applesauce
- 1 egg (use a flax egg to make this recipe vegan)

- ¼ cup ghee, melted
- 1 tsp vanilla extract
- ¼ cup unsweetened almond milk

Directions

1. Spray a silicone muffin pan with non-stick cooking oil and set aside.
2. Combine the frozen blueberries, cassava flour, coconut sugar, salt, and baking powder in a large mixing bowl. Stir to combine.
3. Next, combine the applesauce, egg, ghee, vanilla extract, and unsweetened almond milk in a small mixing bowl and stir to combine.
4. Pour the wet mixture into the dry mixture and stir to combine.
5. Use a TBSP to fill the muffin wells ¾ of the way full.
6. Place the muffin pan on the tray of your air fryer. Set the temperature to 360° for 10 minutes.
7. When the cooking time is up, remove the muffin tin and transfer the muffins to a cooling rack.
8. Next, use your spoon to divide the rest of the batter into the muffin pan and repeat the baking process.
9. Serve warm, and refrigerate or freeze any leftover muffins.

Nutritional Facts:

- Calories: 210
- Fat: 8 g
- Carbohydrates: 27 g
- Protein: 3 g

Chocolate Lava Cake

Serves: 2

Cook Time: 10 minutes

Ingredients

- 1 egg
- 2 TBSP cocoa powder
- 2 TBSP water
- 2 TBSP non-GMO erythritol
- 1/8 tsp Now Brand Better Stevia
- 1 TBSP golden flaxmeal
- 1 TBSP coconut oil, melted
- ½ tsp aluminum-free baking powder

- Dash of vanilla
- Pinch of Himalayan salt

Directions

1. Whisk all ingredients in a two-cup glass Pyrex dish or ramekin.
2. Preheat air fryer at 350° for just a minute.
3. Place glass dish with cake mix into air fryer and bake at 350° for 8-9 minutes.
4. Carefully remove dish with an oven mitt.
5. Let cool for a few minutes and then enjoy!

Nutritional Facts:

- Calories: 173
- Fat: 13 g
- Carbohydrates: 4 g
- Protein: 8 g

Air Fryer Steak Tips

Serves: 3

Cook Time: 10 minutes

Ingredients

- 1.5 lb steak (Ribeye, New York) or beef chuck for a cheaper version cut to 3/4 inch cubes

AIR FRYER STEAK MARINADE

- 1 tsp oil
- ½ tsp salt
- ½ tsp black pepper, freshly ground
- ½ tsp dried garlic powder

- ½ tsp dried onion powder
- 1/8 tsp cayenne pepper

AIR FRYER ASPARAGUS

- 1 lb asparagus, tough ends trimmed
- ¼ tsp salt
- ½ tsp oil (optional)

Directions

1. Preheat the air fryer at 400°F for about 5 minutes.
2. Meanwhile, trim the steak of any fat and cut it into cubes. Then, toss with the ingredients for the marinade (oil, salt, black pepper, onion, garlic powder, and the cayenne pepper) and massage the spices into the meat to coat evenly. Do this in a ziplock bag for easier cleanup.
3. Spray the bottom of the air fryer basket with nonstick spray if you have any and spread the prepared meat along the bottom of it. Cook the beef steak tips for about 4-6 minutes and check for desired cook.
4. Toss the asparagus with ½ tsp oil and ¼ tsp salt until evenly coated.
5. Once the steak bites are browned to your liking, toss them around and move to one side. Add the asparagus

to the other side of the air fryer basket and cook for another 3 minutes.

6. Remove the steak tips and the asparagus to a serving plate and serve while hot.

Nutritional Facts:
- Calories: 526
- Fat: 34 g
- Carbohydrates: 6 g
- Protein: 50 g

Perfect Onion Rings

Serves: 4

Cook Time: 5 minutes

Ingredients

- 1 cup buttermilk
- ½ cup breadcrumbs
- 1 cup flour
- 1 TBSP of Parmesan cheese
- 1 egg
- 1 tsp salt
- 1 tsp pepper
- 2 large onions, cut into rings

- Non-stick cooking spray

Directions

1. Combine the buttermilk and egg. Mix well.
2. In another bowl combine the breadcrumbs, flour, Parmesan cheese, salt, and pepper. Mix well.
3. Dip the onions into the buttermilk/egg mixture and then dip into the flour mixture. Then place them on a baking sheet lined with parchment paper, refrigerate them for 30 minutes.
4. Then set your temperature to 400°F. Set, the timer for 2 minutes, then flip them over and do another 2 minutes.
5. Repeat until they are all done.

Nutritional Facts:

- Calories: 114
- Fat: 1 g
- Carbohydrates: 18 g
- Protein: 5 g

Crunchy Parmesan Chickpeas

Serves: 4

Cook Time: 15 minutes

Ingredients

- 2 (15 oz) cans chickpeas, drained and patted completely dry
- 2 TBSP olive oil
- ¼ cup grated (crumbly) Parmesan cheese
- 1 tsp garlic powder
- Zest of one lemon
- 1 tsp dried oregano leaves
- 1 tsp kosher salt

- ½ tsp coarsely ground black pepper

Directions

1. Drain and rinse your chickpeas under cold water, patting completely dry with a paper towel.
2. Combine all ingredients in a large bowl and toss gently until chickpeas are covered uniformly in seasonings.
3. Set air fryer to 390°F. Divide chickpeas into three batches, air frying one batch at a time so as to not overcrowd them. Air fry for 5-6 minutes, remove and shake the basket and air fry for another 5 minutes or until desired crispiness is reached. Repeat with each batch until done.
4. Serve immediately over cool chickpeas in a single layer on paper towels or parchment sheets before storing in parchment bags for up to three days.

Nutritional Facts:

- Calories: 251
- Fat: 6 g
- Carbohydrates: 36 g
- Protein: 11 g

Chick-Fil-A Chicken Sandwich

Serves: 6

Cook Time: 15 minutes

Ingredients

- 2 chicken breasts boneless/skinless, pounded
- 1/2 cup dill pickle juice
- 2 eggs
- ½ cup milk
- 1 cup all-purpose flour
- 2 TBSP powdered sugar
- 2 TBSP potato starch
- 1 tsp paprika
- 1 tsp sea salt

- ½ tsp freshly ground black pepper
- ½ tsp garlic powder
- ¼ tsp ground celery seed
- 1 TBSP extra virgin olive oil
- 1 oil mister
- 4 hamburger buns toasted/buttered
- 8 dill pickle chips, or more

SPICY OPTION

- ¼ tsp cayenne pepper for spicy sandwiches

Directions

1. Place chicken into a Ziploc baggie and pound, so that the whole piece is the same thickness, about ½-inch thick. Cut chicken into two or three pieces (depending on size).

2. Place pieces of chicken back into Ziploc baggie and pour in pickle juice. Marinate in the refrigerator for at least 30 minutes.

3. In a medium bowl, beat egg with the milk. In another bowl, combine flour, starch, and all spices.

4. Using tongs, coat chicken with egg mixture and then into flour mixture, making sure pieces are completely coated. Shake off excess flour (this is important).

Spray the basket of your air fryer with oil and place chicken into air fryer and spray the chicken with oil.

5. Cook at 340° for 6 minutes. Using silicone tongs, carefully flip the chicken and spray with oil. Cook for 6 more minutes.

6. Raise the temperature to 400° and cook for two minutes on each side.

7. Serve on buttered and toasted buns, with 2 pickle chips and a small dollop of mayonnaise, if desired.

Nutritional Facts:

- Calories: 281
- Fat: 6 g
- Carbohydrates: 36 g
- Protein: 15 g

Pork Taquitos

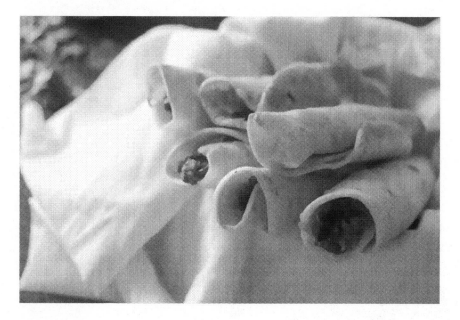

Serves: 10

Cook Time: 12 minutes

Ingredients
- 3 cups cooked shredded pork tenderloin or chicken
- 2 ½ cups fat-free shredded mozzarella
- 10 small flour tortillas
- 1 lime, juiced
- Cooking spray

Directions
1. Preheat air fryer to 380°.
2. Sprinkle lime juice over pork and gently mix around.

3. Microwave 5 tortillas at a time with a damp paper towel over it for 10 seconds, to soften.

4. Add 3 oz of pork and ¼ cup of cheese to a tortilla.

5. Tightly and gently roll up the tortillas.

6. Line tortillas on a greased foil-lined pan.

7. Spray an even coat of cooking spray over tortillas.

8. Air fry for 7-10 minutes until tortillas are a golden color, flipping halfway through.

Nutritional Facts:

- Calories: 256
- Fat: 4 g
- Carbohydrates: 23 g
- Protein: 30 g

Conclusion

I hope you enjoyed our **"Easy Air Fryer Cookbook: 69 Delicious Recipes for Fast and Healthy Meals."**

An air fryer is essentially a revolutionized kitchen appliance for cooking various foods through the dissemination of superheated air.

It is another advanced development from the top-notch kitchen device experts that offers healthy, quality food with less oil.

Thanks again for downloading this book; I hope you enjoyed it!